Learn to Write the Alphabet - All Animals

The Danger Twins Writing Series

ISBN PAPERBACK: 978-1-956547-04-7

Book design by Anne Lusher

Published by Unplanned Books, LLC.

UNPLANNED BOOKS

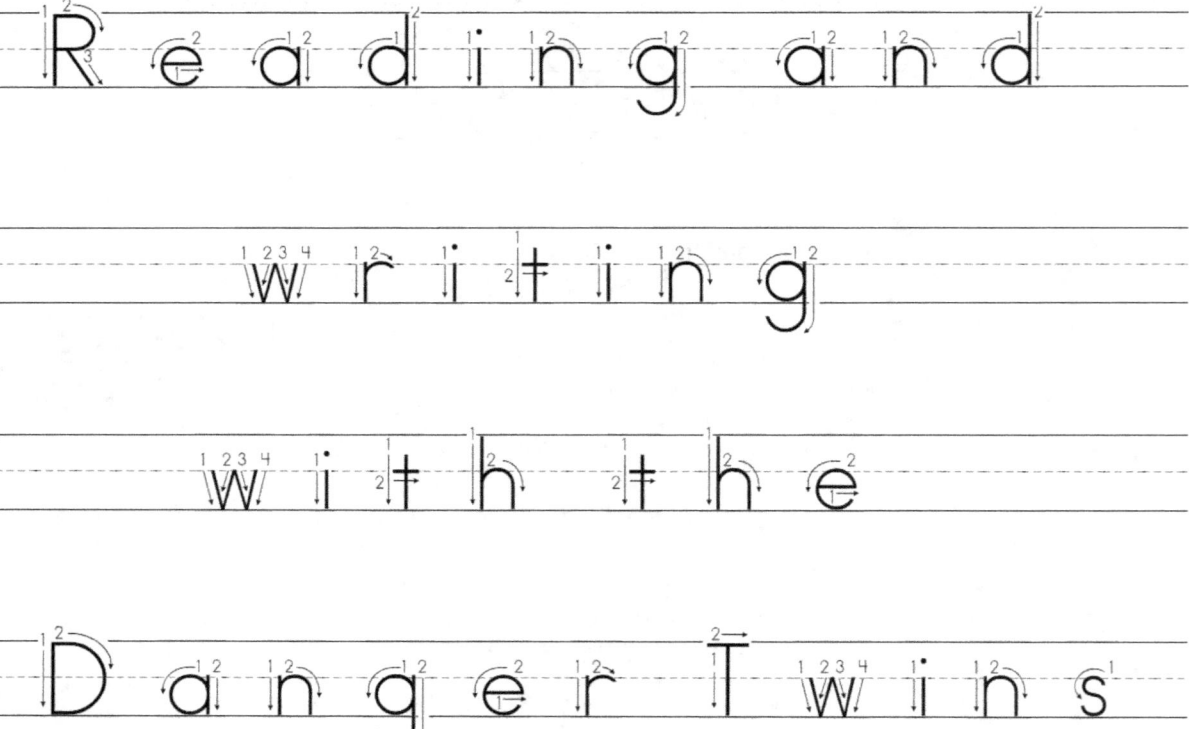

Reading and
writing
with the
Danger Twins

Trace the individual letters.
Then trace each animal name
and then say it aloud.

A A A A A A A A

A A A A A A A A

a a a a a a a a

Alligator

Alligator Alligator

Alpaca

Alpaca Alpaca

3

Trace the individual letters.
Then trace each animal name
and then say it aloud.

B B B B B B B

B B B B B B B

b b b b b b b

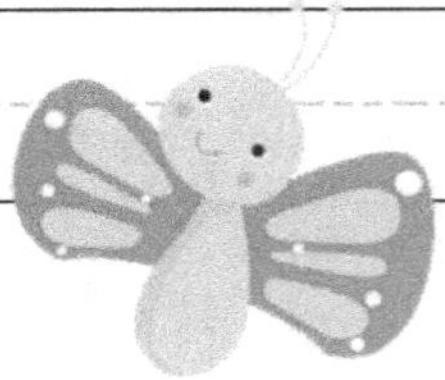

Butterfly

Butterfly Butterfly

Buffalo

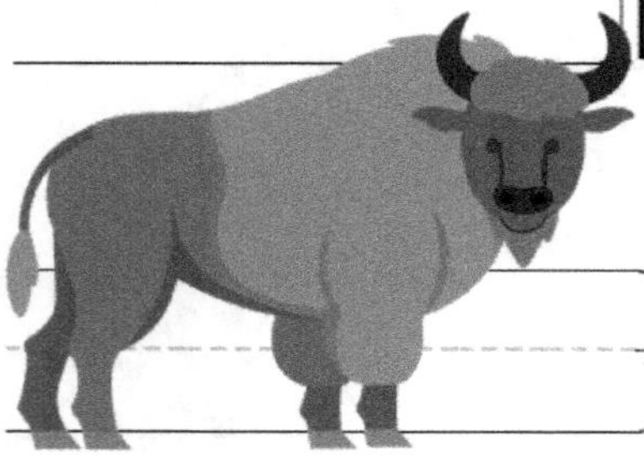

Buffalo Buffalo

4

WRITING WITH THE DANGER TWINS

C¹ C c¹

Trace the individual letters.
Then trace each animal name
and then say it aloud.

C C C C C

C C C C C

c c c c c c

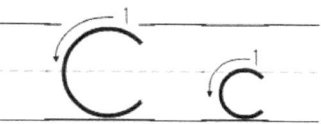

C¹ a¹² t¹²

Cat Cat

C¹ o¹ y¹² o¹ t¹² e²

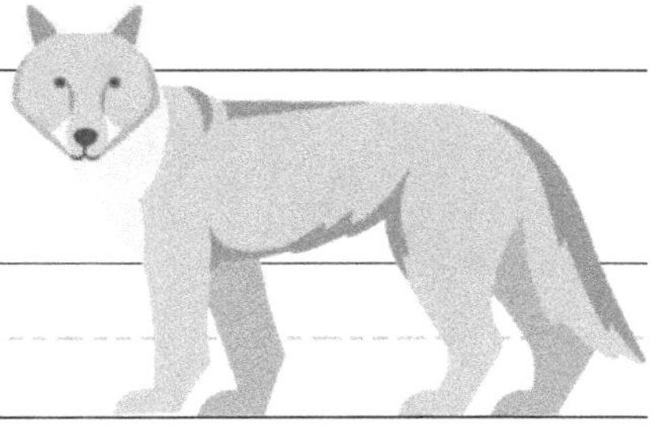

Coyote Coyote

WRITING WITH THE DANGER TWINS

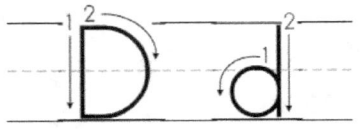

Trace the individual letters. Then trace each animal name and then say it aloud.

D D D D D D D

D D D D D D D

d d d d d d d

D o l p h i n

Dolphin Dolphin

D e e r

Deer Deer

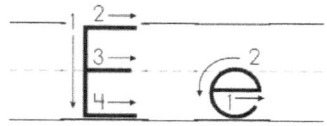

Trace the individual letters.
Then trace each animal name
and then say it aloud.

E E E E E E E

E E E E E E E

e e e e e e e

E l e p h a n t

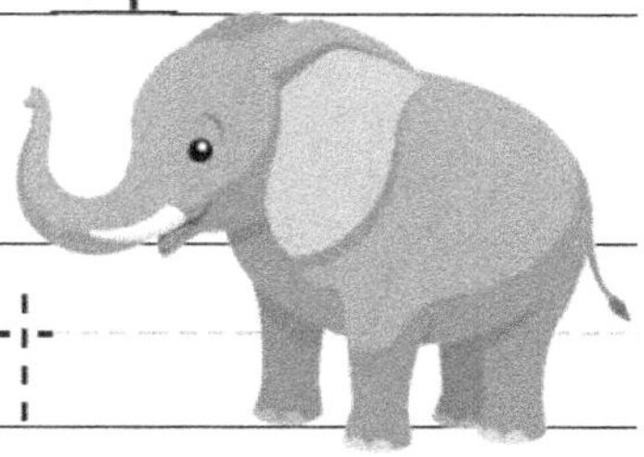

Elephant Elephant

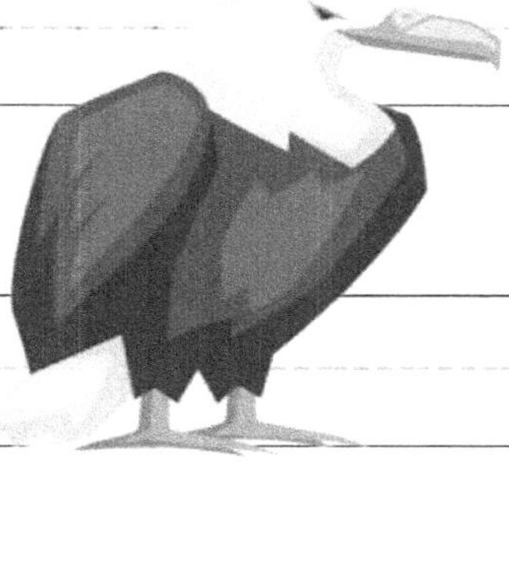

E a g l e

Eagle Eagle

7

WRITING WITH THE DANGER TWINS

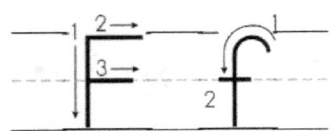

Trace the individual letters.
Then trace each animal name
and then say it aloud.

F F F F F F

F F F F F F

f f f f f f f

Flamingo

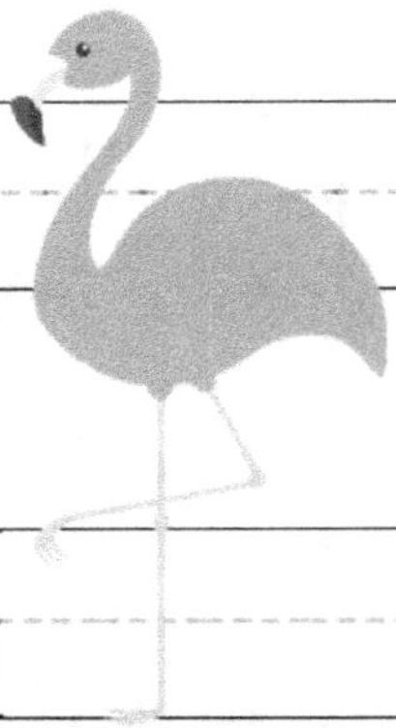

Flamingo   Flamingo

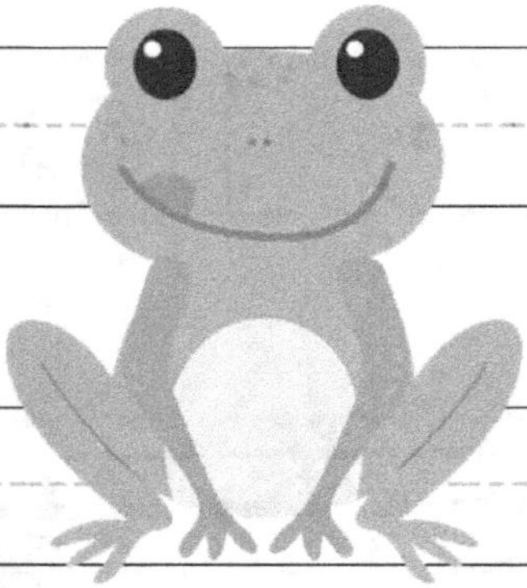

Frog

Frog   Frog

WRITING WITH THE DANGER TWINS

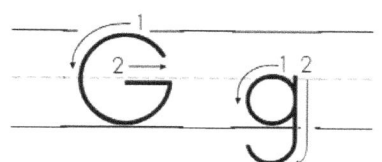

Trace the individual letters.
Then trace each animal name
and then say it aloud.

G G G G G G G

G G G G G

g g g g g g g g

Giraffe

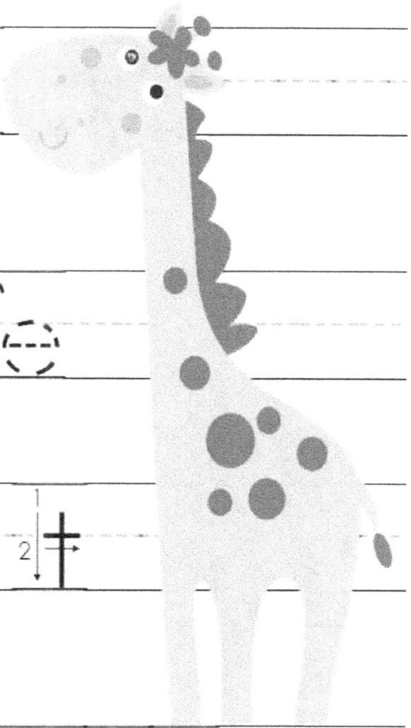

Giraffe Giraffe

Goat

Goat Goat

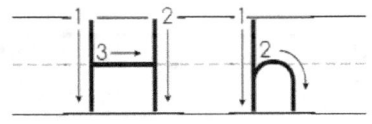

Trace the individual letters.
Then trace each animal name
and then say it aloud.

H H H H H H H H

H H H H H H H H

h h h h h h h h

Hippopotamus

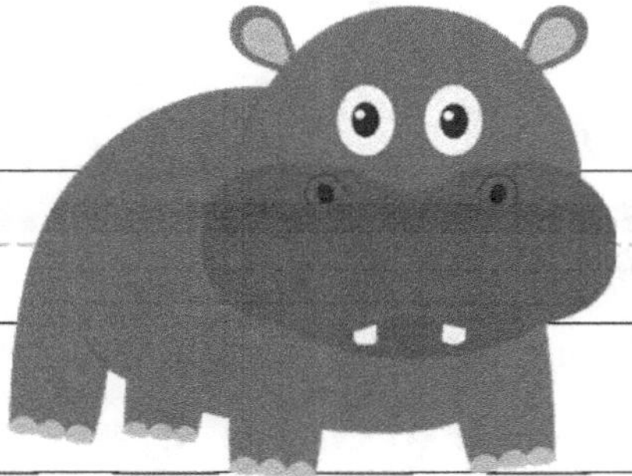

Hippo Hippo

Hamster

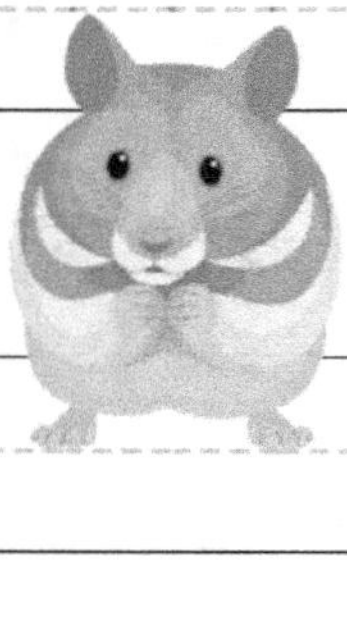

Hamster Hamster

10

Trace the individual letters.
Then trace each animal name
and then say it aloud.

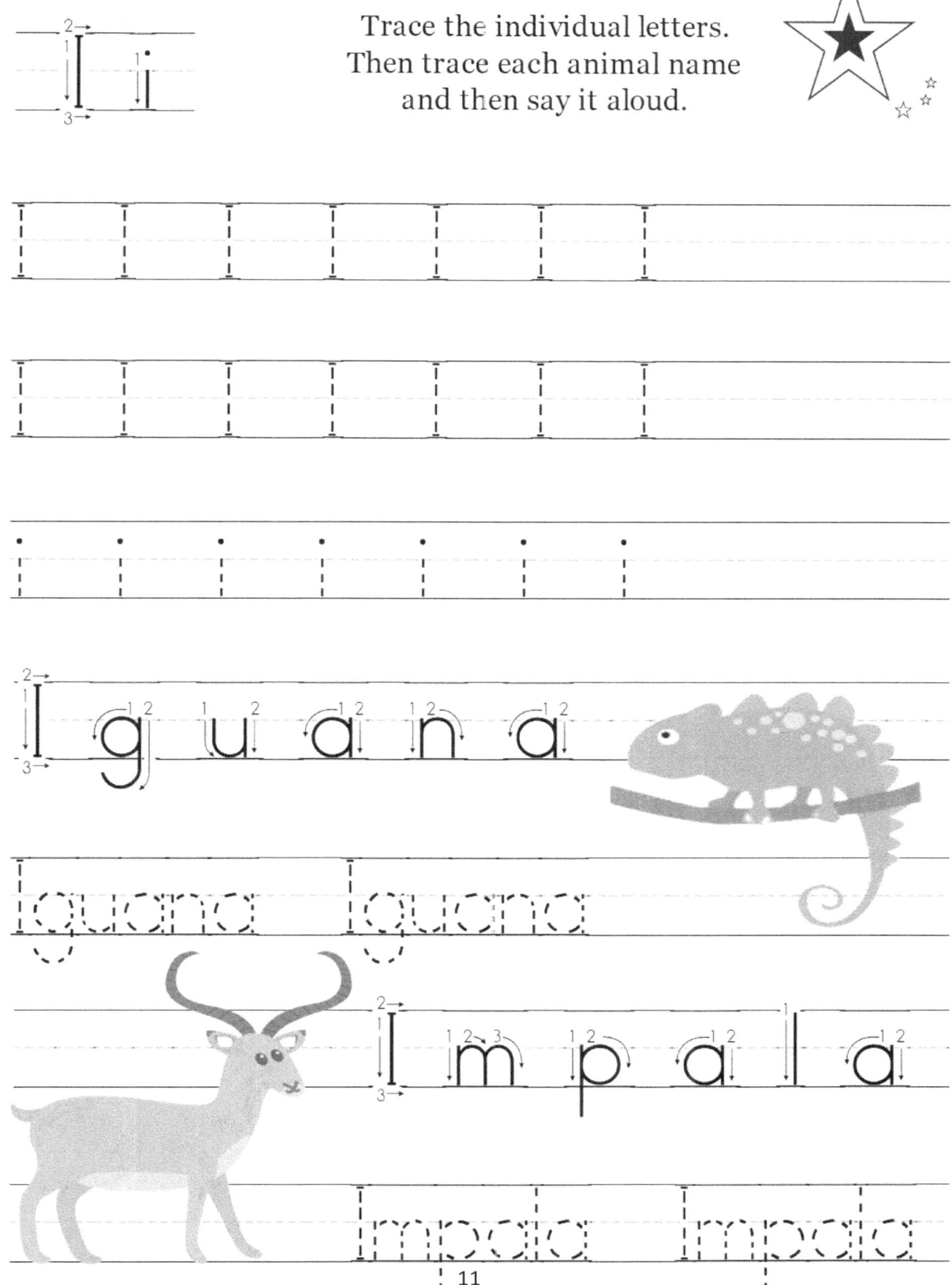

Iguana   Iguana

Impala   Impala

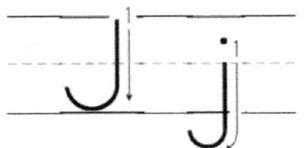

Trace the individual letters.
Then trace each animal name
and then say it aloud.

J J J J J J J J

J J J J J J J J

j j j j j j j j

Jellyfish

Jellyfish   Jellyfish

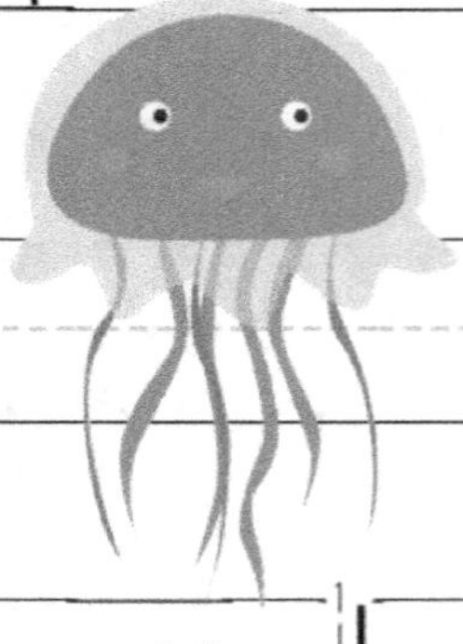

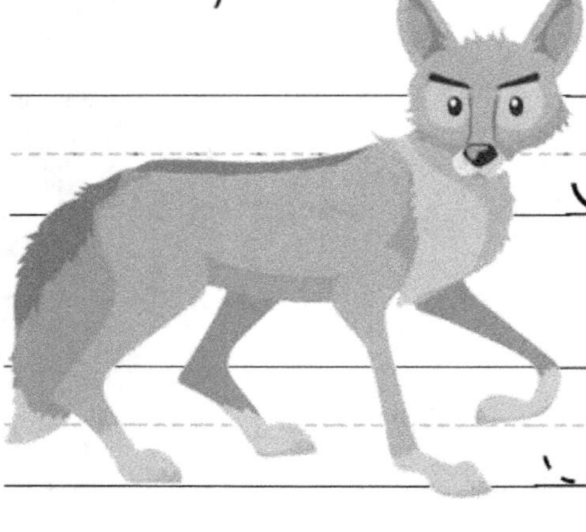

Jackal

Jackal   Jackal

WRITING WITH THE DANGER TWINS

Trace the individual letters. Then trace each animal name and then say it aloud.

K K K K K K K

K K K K K K K

k k k k k k k

Koala

Koala koala

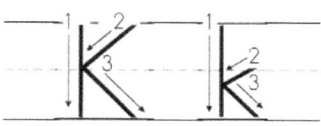

Kiwi

Kiwi Kiwi

WRITING WITH THE DANGER TWINS

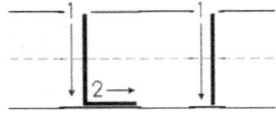

Trace the individual letters.
Then trace each animal name
and then say it aloud.

L L L L L L L

L L L L L L L

l l l l l l l l l l

Lion

Lion Lion

Lamb

Lamb Lamb

WRITING WITH THE DANGER TWINS

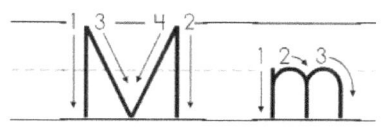

Trace the individual letters. Then trace each animal name and then say it aloud.

M M M M M

M M M M M

m m m m m m

Mouse

Mouse   Mouse

Moose

Moose Moose

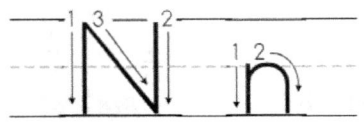

Trace the individual letters.
Then trace each animal name
and then say it aloud.

N N N N N N

N N N N N N

n n n n n n n

Narwhal

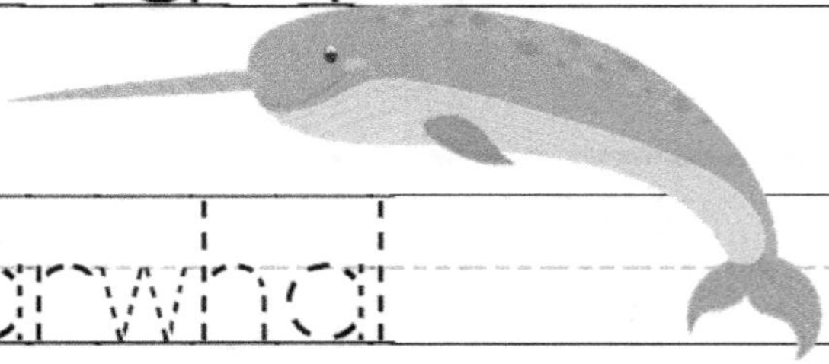

Narwhal Narwhal

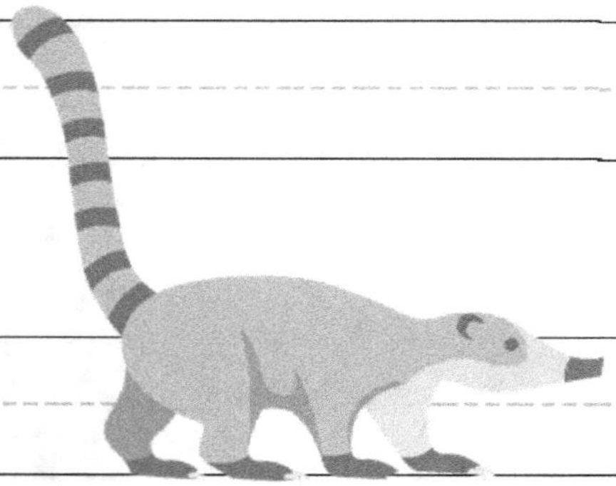

Nasua

Nasua Nasua

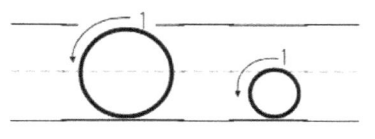

Trace the individual letters.
Then trace each animal name
and then say it aloud.

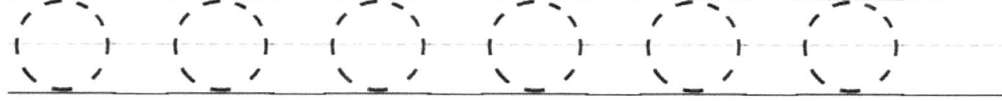

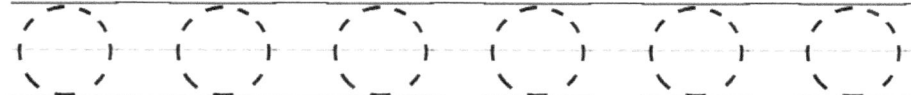

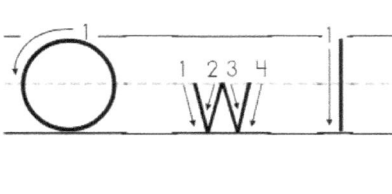

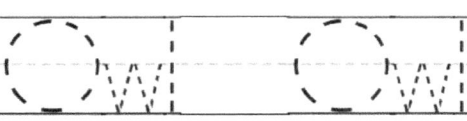

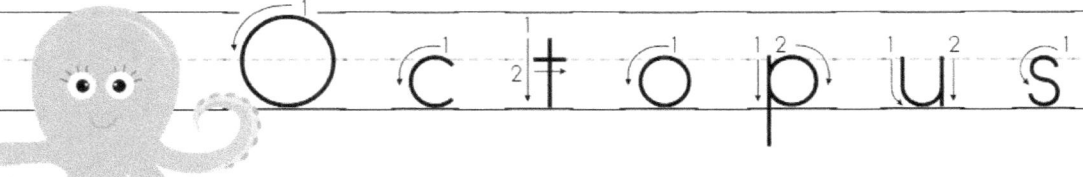

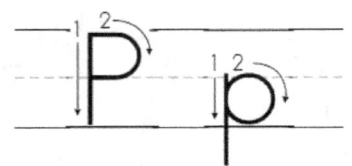

Trace the individual letters.
Then trace each animal name
and then say it aloud.

P P P P P P P

P P P P P P P

P P P P P P P

Panda

Panda Panda

Pig

Pig Pig

WRITING WITH THE DANGER TWINS

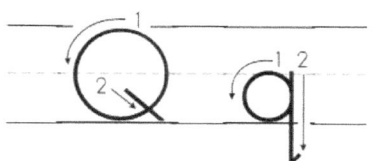

Trace the individual letters. Then trace each animal name and then say it aloud.

Q Q Q Q Q Q

Q Q Q Q Q

q q q q q q q

Quail

Quail Quail

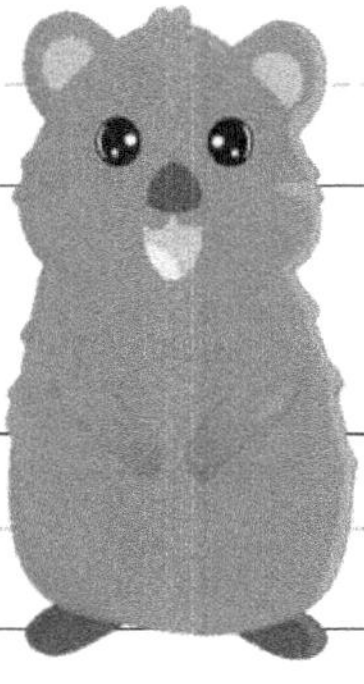

Quokka

Quokka Quokka

WRITING WITH THE DANGER TWINS

R r

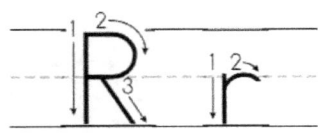

Trace the individual letters.
Then trace each animal name
and then say it aloud.

R R R R R R R

R R R R R R R

r r r r r r r r

Rooster

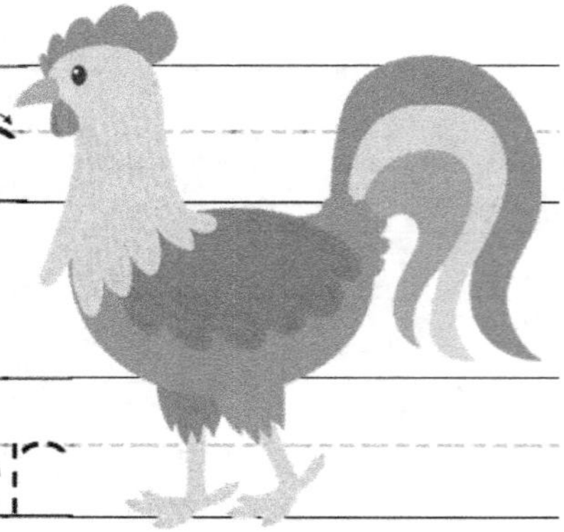

Rooster Rooster

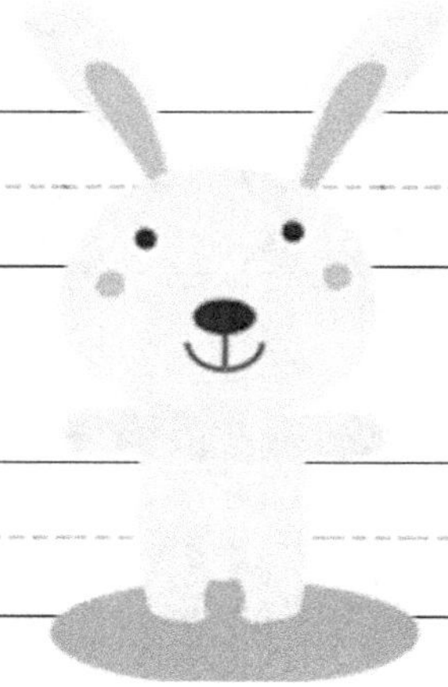

Rabbit

Rabbit Rabbit

WRITING WITH THE DANGER TWINS

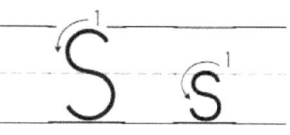

Trace the individual letters. Then trace each animal name and then say it aloud.

S S S S S S

S S S S S S

s s s s s s s

S l o t h

Sloth Sloth

Spider

Spider Spider

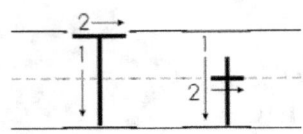

Trace the individual letters.
Then trace each animal name
and then say it aloud.

T T T T T T

T T T T T T

t t t t t t t t

Turtle

Turtle Turtle

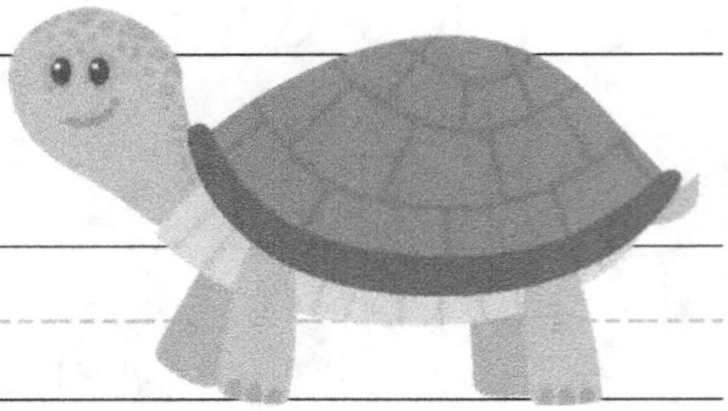

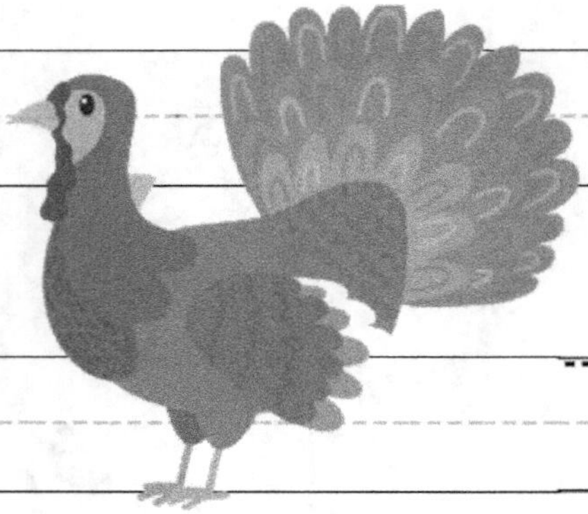

Turkey

Turkey Turkey

WRITING WITH THE DANGER TWINS

U u

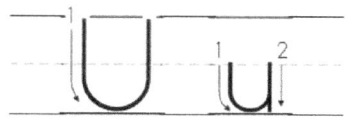

Trace the individual letters.
Then trace each animal name
and then say it aloud.

U U U U U U

U U U U U U

u u u u u u u

Urial

Urial Urial

Unau

Unau Unau

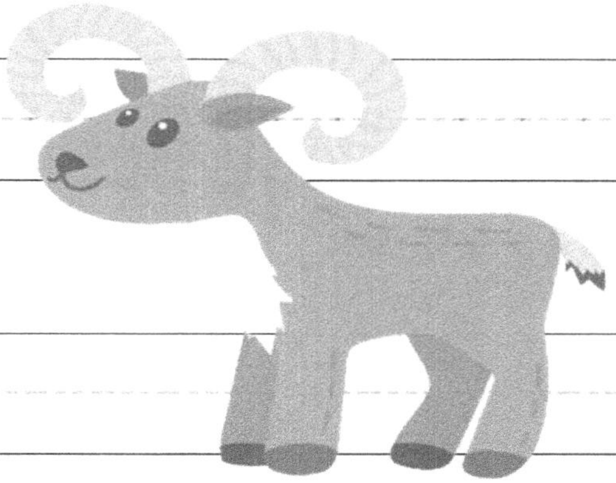

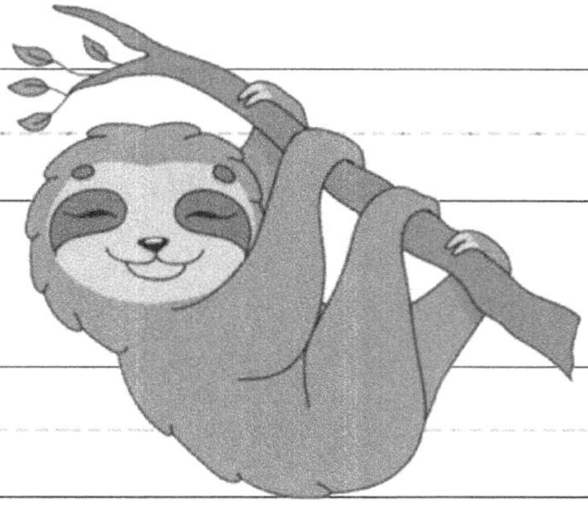

Trace the individual letters.
Then trace each animal name
and then say it aloud.

V v

V V V V V V

V V V V V V

v v v v v v v

Vulture

Vulture Vulture

Vervet

Vervet Vervet

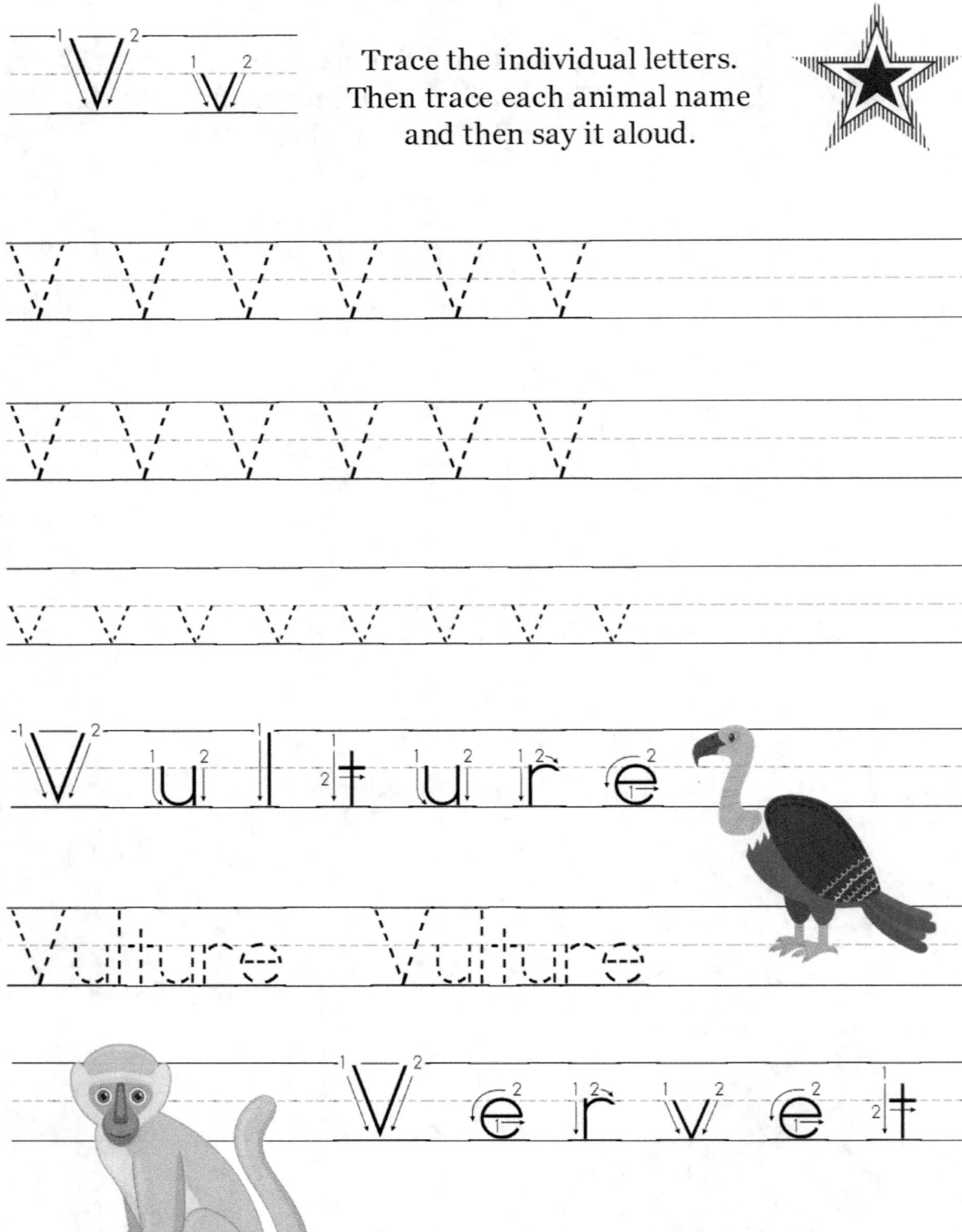

WRITING WITH THE DANGER TWINS

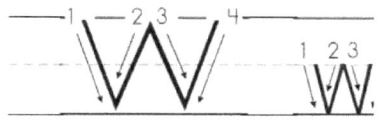

Trace the individual letters. Then trace each animal name and then say it aloud.

W W W W

W W W W

w w w w w w w

Whale

Whale Whale

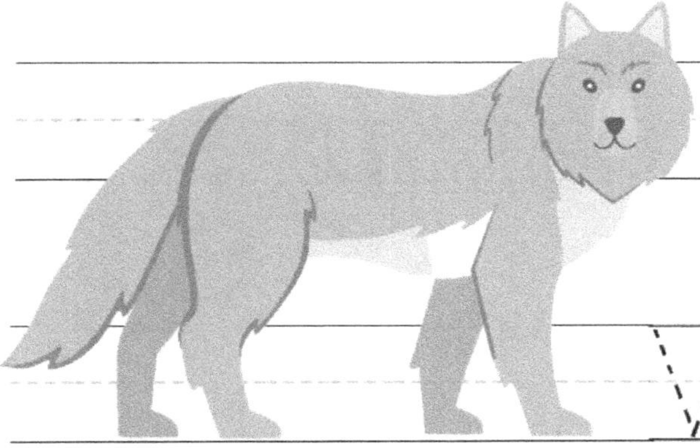

Wolf

Wolf Wolf

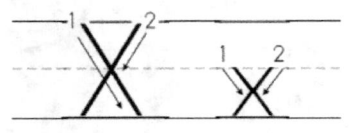

Trace the individual letters.
Then trace each animal name
and then say it aloud.

X X X X X X X X

X X X X X X X X

X X X X X X X

X-ray tetra

X-ray tetra   X-ray tetra

Xerus

Xerus Xerus

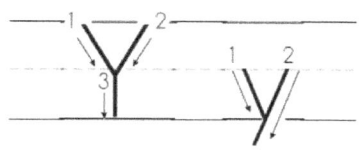

Trace the individual letters.
Then trace each animal name
and then say it aloud.

Y Y Y Y Y Y Y Y

Y Y Y Y Y Y Y Y

y y y y y y y y

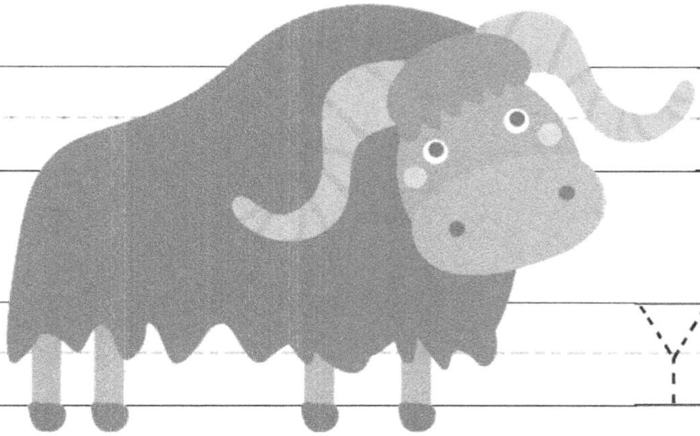

Yak   Yak   Yak

Yurumi

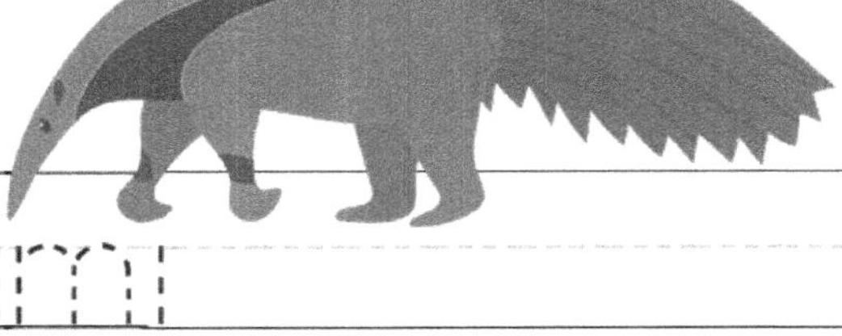

Yurumi   Yurumi

WRITING WITH THE DANGER TWINS

Z z

Trace the individual letters. Then trace each animal name and then say it aloud.

Z Z Z Z Z Z Z

Z Z Z Z Z Z Z

z z z z z z z

Z e b r a

Zebra Zebra

Z u c h o n

Zuchon Zuchon

28

BONUS WORDS FROM THE DANGER TWINS

The Danger Twins listed their favorite animals below. Write your favorite animals from the first section of this book.

Turtle   Yak

Panda   Sloth

WRITING WITH THE DANGER TWINS

A a

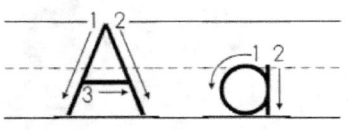

Trace the individual letters.
Then trace each animal name
and then say it aloud.

a a a a a a a a

a a a a a a a a

A A A A A A A

Antelope

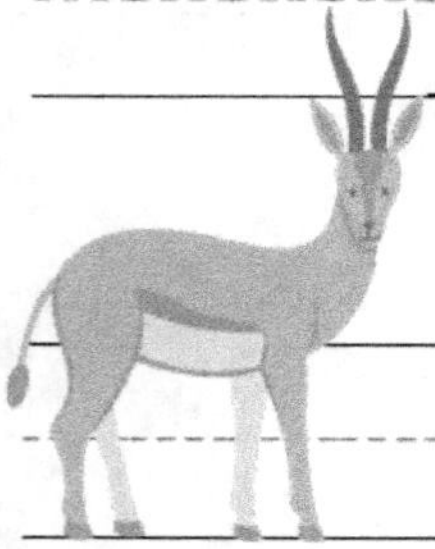

Antelope Antelope

Aardvark

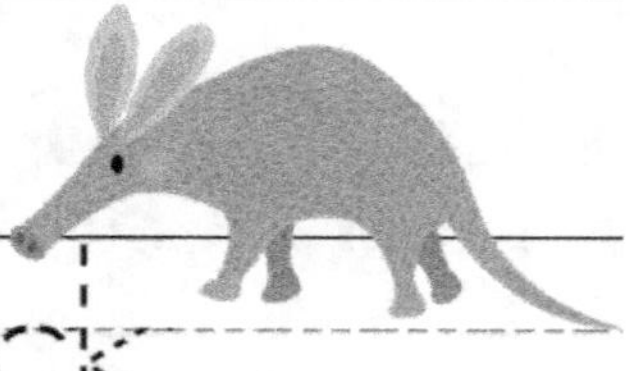

Aardvark Aardvark

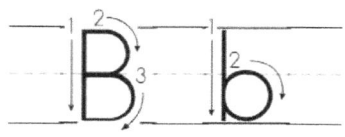

Trace the individual letters.
Then trace each animal name
and then say it aloud.

b b b b b b b

b b b b b b b

B B B B B B B

Blue Whale

Blue Whale

baboon

baboon baboon

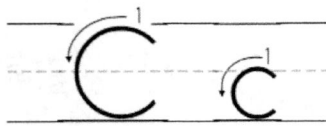

Trace the individual letters.
Then trace each animal name
and then say it aloud.

C C C C C C

C C C C C C

c c c c c

Chicken

Chicken Chicken

Canary

Canary Canary

WRITING WITH THE DANGER TWINS

D d

Trace the individual letters.
Then trace each animal name
and then say it aloud.

d d d d d d d

d d d d d d d

D D D D D D D

Dalmation

Dalmation Dalmation

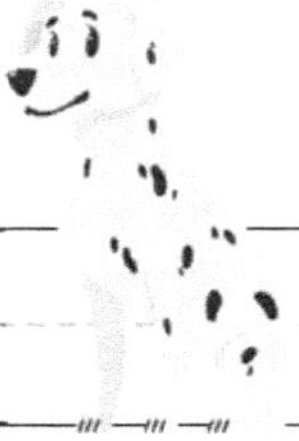

Dingo

Dingo Dingo

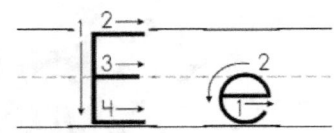

Trace the individual letters.
Then trace each animal name
and then say it aloud.

Elk

Ek

Earthworm

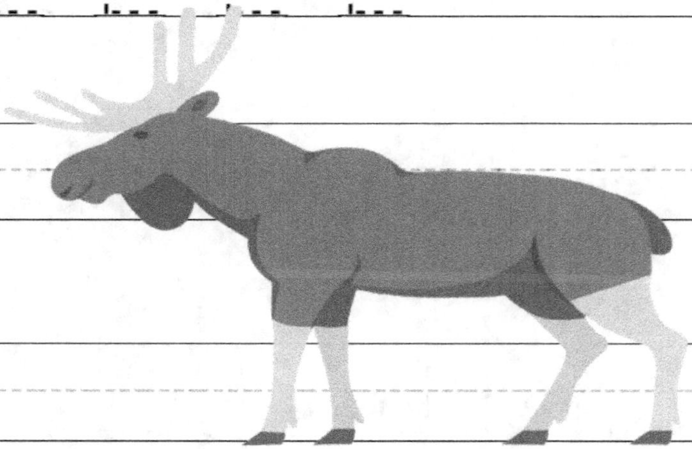

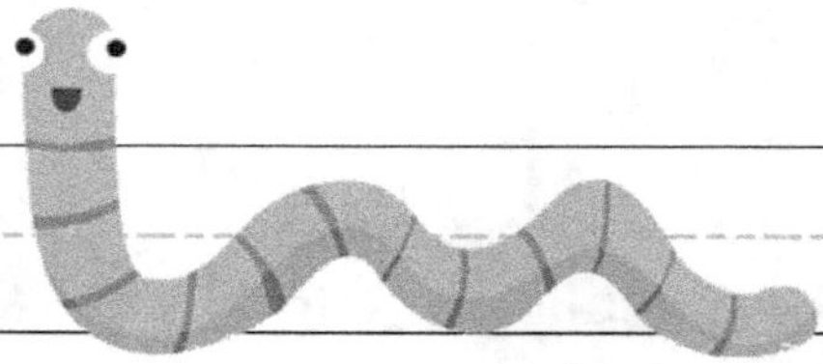

Earthworm

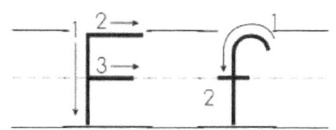

Trace the individual letters.
Then trace each animal name
and then say it aloud.

f f f f f f f

f f f f f f f

F F F F F F F

Fox

Fox Fox

Ferret

Ferret Ferret

WRITING WITH THE DANGER TWINS

G g

Trace the individual letters.
Then trace each animal name
and then say it aloud.

g g g g g g g

g g g g g g g

G G G G G

Gorilla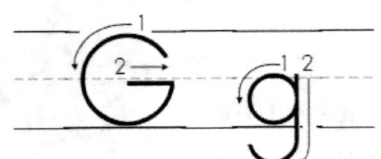

Gorilla   Gorilla

Grasshopper

Grasshopper

36

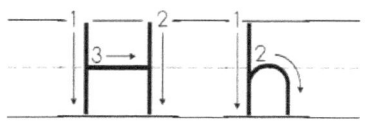

Trace the individual letters.
Then trace each animal name
and then say it aloud.

h h h h h h

h h h h h h

H H H H H H

Hedgehog

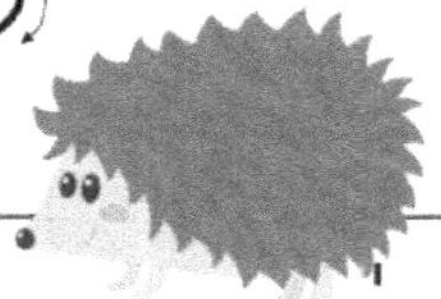

Hedgehog   Hedgehog

Hornbill

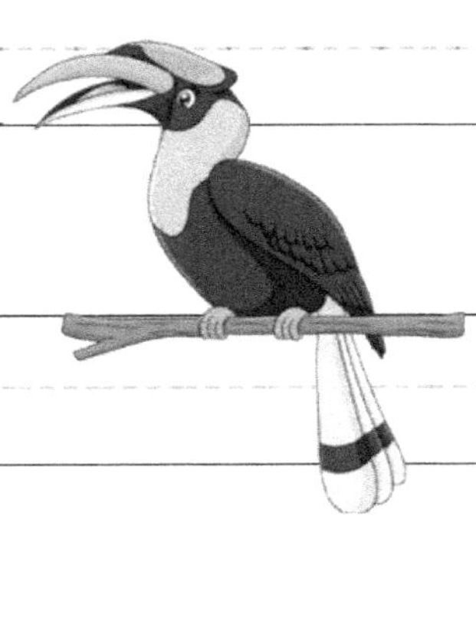

Hornbill   Hornbill

WRITING WITH THE DANGER TWINS

I i

Trace the individual letters.
Then trace each animal name
and then say it aloud.

i i i i i i i i i i

i i i i i i i i i i

I I I I I I

Ibis

Ibis Ibis

Ibex

Ibex Ibex

J j

Trace the individual letters.
Then trace each animal name
and then say it aloud.

j j j j j j j j

j j j j j j j j

J J J J J J

Jaguar

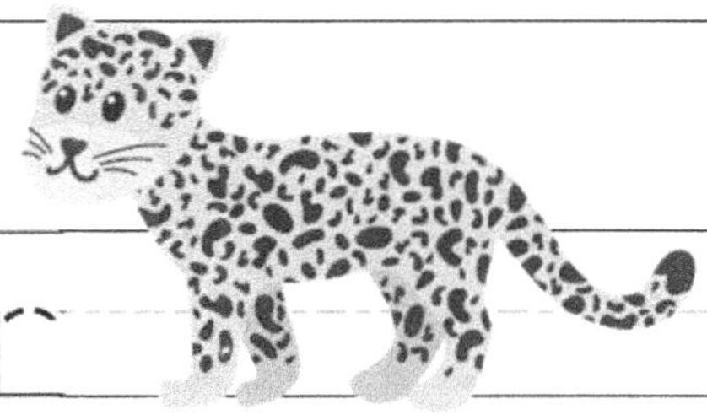

Jaguar   Jaguar

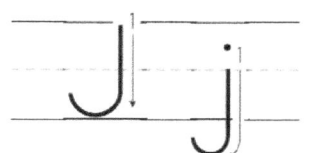

Junglefowl

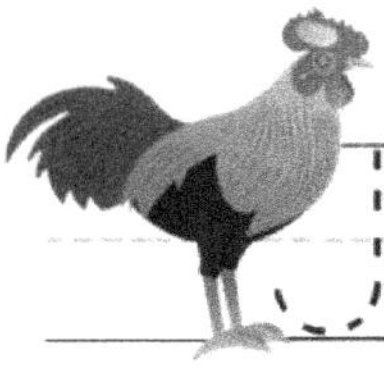

Junglefowl   Junglefowl

WRITING WITH THE DANGER TWINS

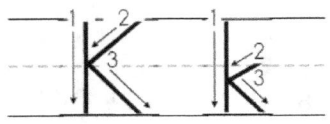

Trace the individual letters.
Then trace each animal name
and then say it aloud.

K K K K K K K K

K K K K K K K K

K K K K K K

Kangaroo

Kangaroo   Kangaroo

Kestrel

Kestrel   Kestrel

WRITING WITH THE DANGER TWINS

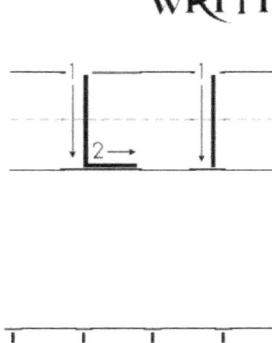

Trace the individual letters.
Then trace each animal name
and then say it aloud.

Lizard

Lizard Lizard

Lobster

Lobster Lobster

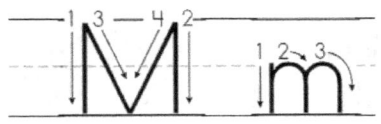

Trace the individual letters.
Then trace each animal name
and then say it aloud.

m m m m m m

m m m m m m

M M M M M

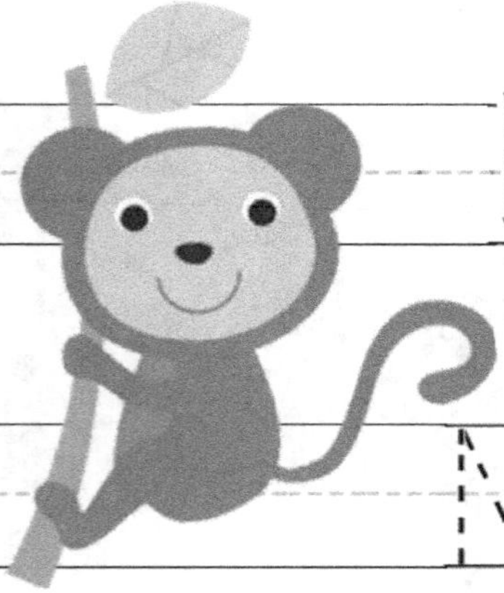

Monkey

Monkey Monkey

Meerkat

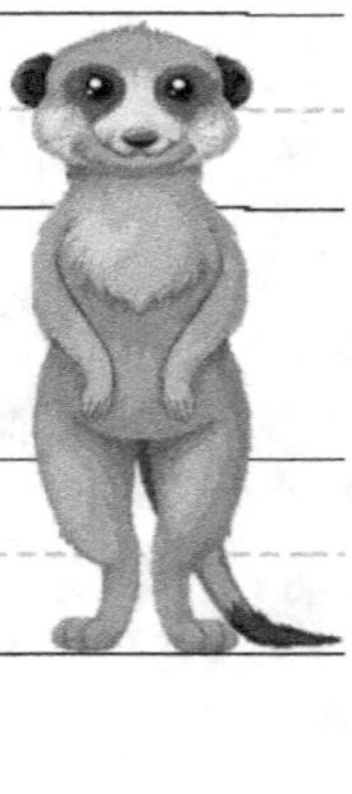

Meerkat Meerkat

WRITING WITH THE DANGER TWINS

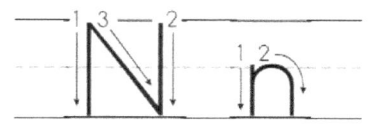

Trace the individual letters. Then trace each animal name and then say it aloud.

n n n n n n n n n

n n n n n n n n n

N N N N N N N

Numbat

Numbat Numbat

Nutria

Nutria Nutria

WRITING WITH THE DANGER TWINS

Trace the individual letters. Then trace each animal name and then say it aloud.

O o

O O O O O O O

O O O O O O O

O O O O O

O s t r i c h

Ostrich Ostrich

O p o s s u m

Opossum Opossum

44

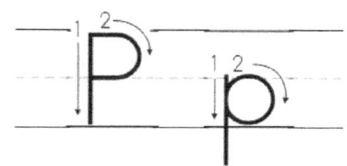

Trace the individual letters.
Then trace each animal name
and then say it aloud.

P P P P P P

P P P P P P

P P P P P P

Penguin

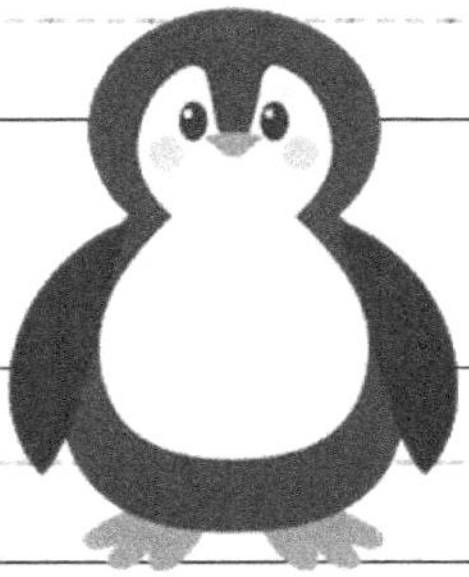

Penguin Penguin

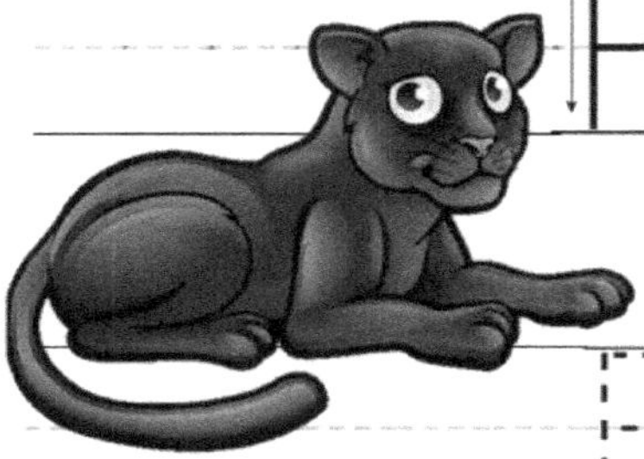

Panther

Panther Panther

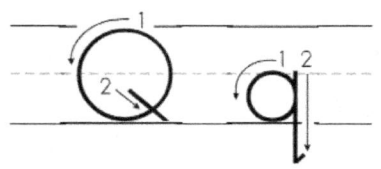

Trace the individual letters.
Then trace each animal name
and then say it aloud.

q q q q q q

q q q q q q

Q Q Q Q Q Q

Quetzal

Quetzal Quetzal

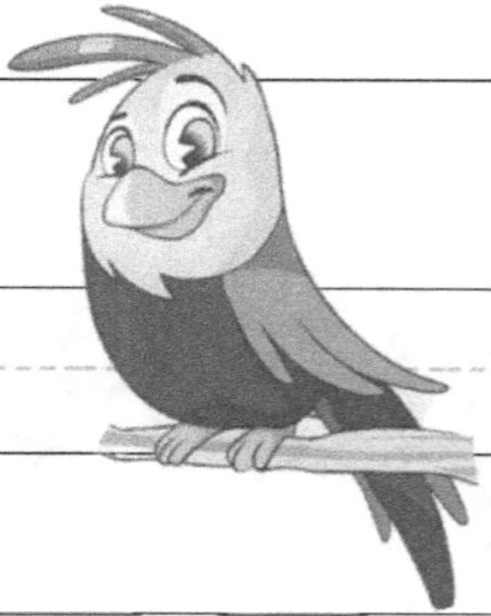

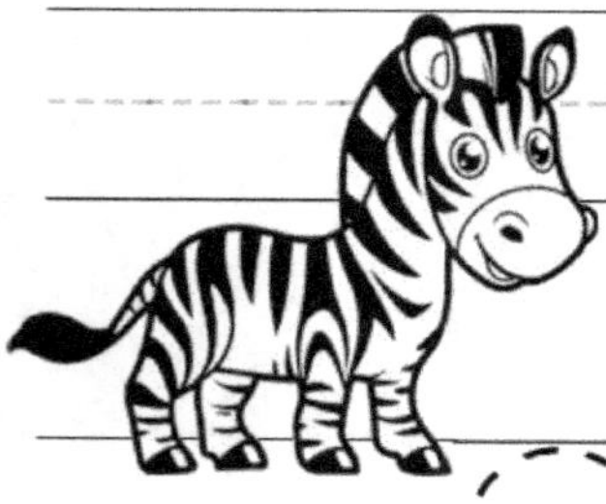

Quagga

Quagga Quagga

Trace the individual letters.
Then trace each animal name
and then say it aloud.

r r r r r r r r

r r r r r r r r

R R R R R R R

Raccoon

Raccoon   Raccoon

Raven

Raven   Raven

47

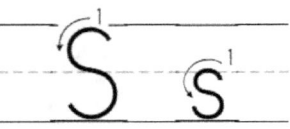

Trace the individual letters.
Then trace each animal name
and then say it aloud.

S s S S S S S S S

S S S S S S S S

S S S S S S

Squirrel

Squirrel Squirrel

Seal

Seal Seal

WRITING WITH THE DANGER TWINS

Trace the individual letters.
Then trace each animal name
and then say it aloud.

Tiger

Tiger Tiger

Toucan

Toucan Toucan

WRITING WITH THE DANGER TWINS

U u

Trace the individual letters.
Then trace each animal name
and then say it aloud.

U U U U U U U

u u u u u u u

U U U U U U

Unicorn

Unicorn Unicorn

Uguisu

Uguisu Uguisu

50

Trace the individual letters.
Then trace each animal name
and then say it aloud.

V v

V V V V V V V V

V V V V V V V V

V V V V V V

Vizsla

Vizsla Vizsla

Vicuna

Vicuna Vicuna

51

WRITING WITH THE DANGER TWINS

Trace the individual letters. Then trace each animal name and then say it aloud.

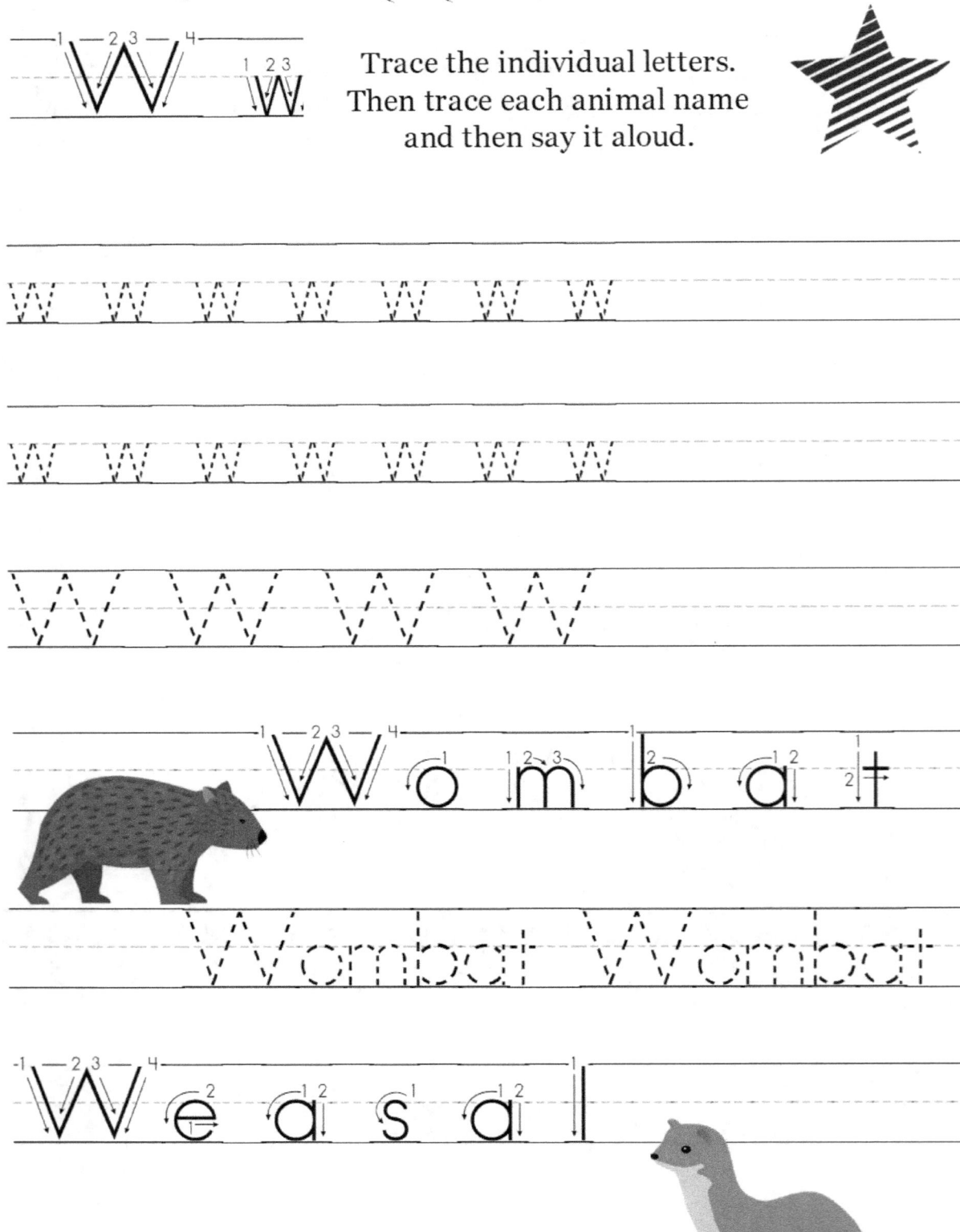

W W W W W W W

W W W W W W W

W W W W

Wombat

Wombat Wombat

Weasal

Weasel Weasel

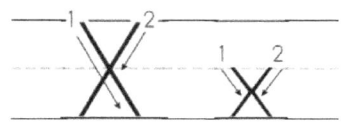

Trace the individual letters.
Then trace each animal name
and then say it aloud.

X X X X X X X

X X X X X X X

X X X X X X

X e m e

Xeme Xeme

X a n t u s

Xantus Xantus

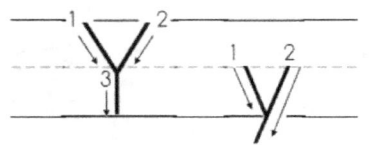

Trace the individual letters.
Then trace each animal name
and then say it aloud.

Y Y Y Y Y Y Y

Y Y Y Y Y Y Y

Y Y Y Y Y

Yorkshire

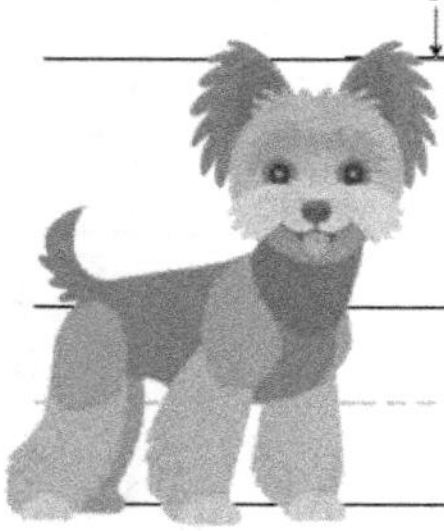

Yorkshire Yorkshire

Yellowfin

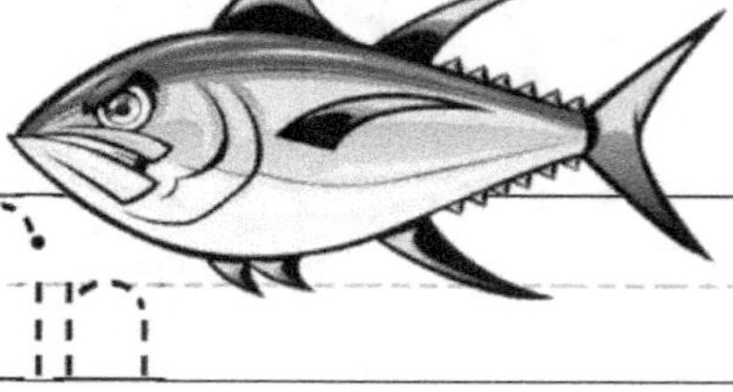

Yellowfin Yellowfin

WRITING WITH THE DANGER TWINS

Zz

Trace the individual letters.
Then trace each animal name
and then say it aloud.

Z Z Z Z Z Z Z

Z Z Z Z Z Z Z

Z Z Z Z Z Z Z

Zonkey

Zonkey Zonkey

Zebu

Zebu Zebu

55

BONUS WORDS FROM THE DANGER TWINS

The Danger Twins listed
their favorite animals below.
Write your favorite animals
from the first section of this book.

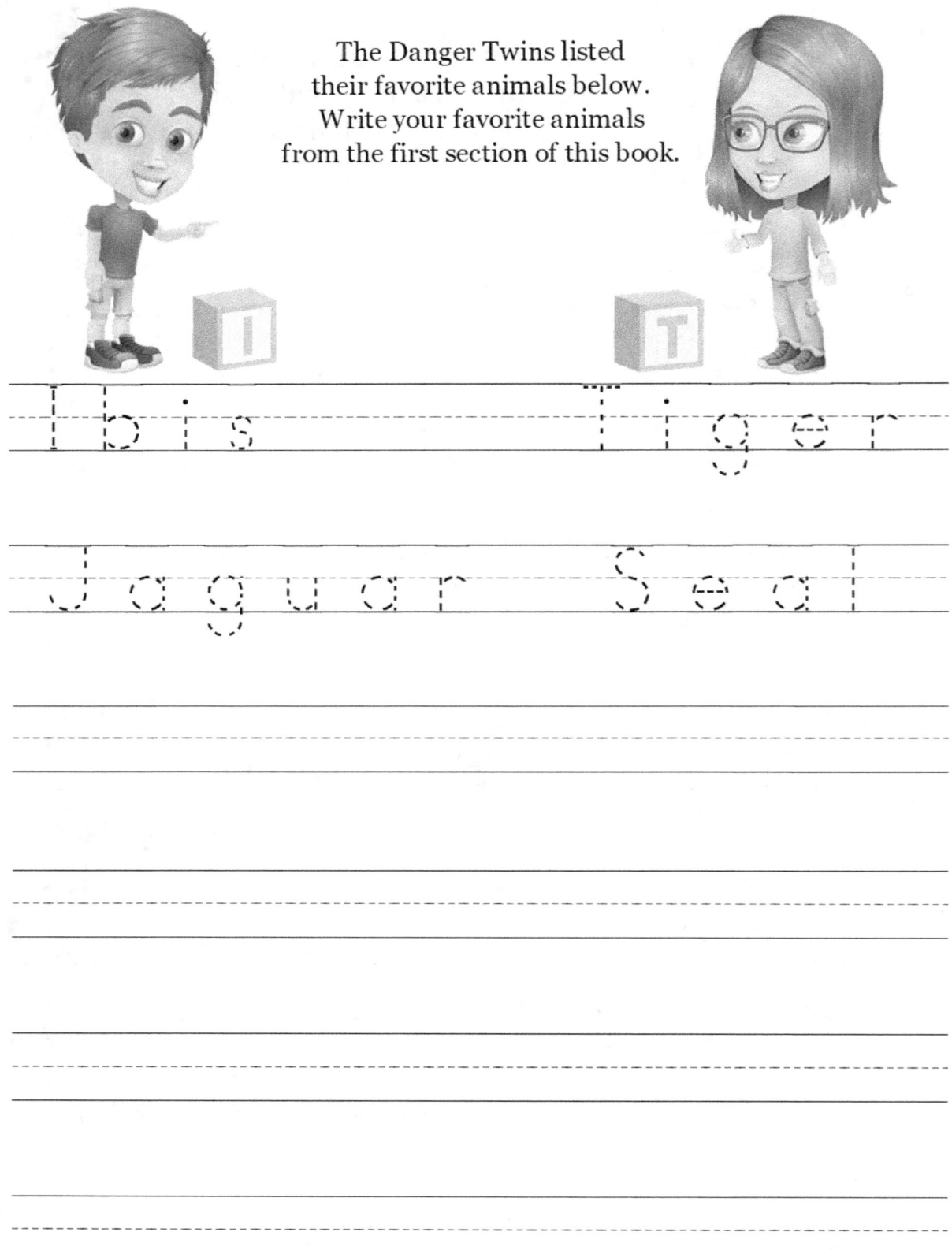

Ibis

Tiger

Jaguar

Seal

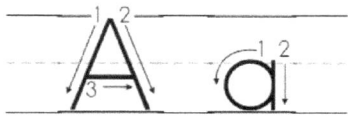

Trace the individual letters.
Then trace each animal name
and then say it aloud.

A A A A A A A A

A

a a a a a a a a

a

A n t e a t e r

Anteater Anteater

A n t Ant Ant

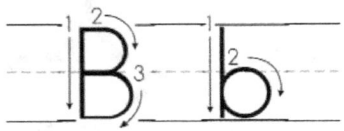

Trace the individual letters.
Then trace each animal name
and then say it aloud.

B B B B B B B

B

b b b b b b b

b

B e a r

Bear Bear

B e e Bee Bee

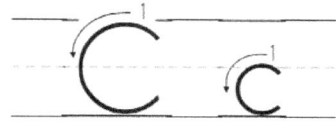

Trace the individual letters.
Then trace each animal name
and then say it aloud.

C C C C C

C

c c c c c c

c

Camel

Camel   Camel

Cow   Cow

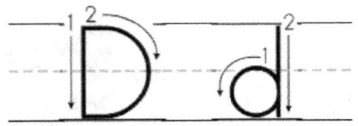

Trace the individual letters.
Then trace each animal name
and then say it aloud.

D D D D D D

D

d d d d d d

d

Donkey

Donkey Donkey

Dodo Dodo

WRITING WITH THE DANGER TWINS

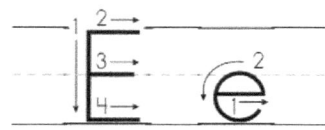

Trace the individual letters.
Then trace each animal name
and then say it aloud.

E E E E E E E

E

e e e e e e e

e

E l a n d

Eland Eland

E m u   Emu Emu

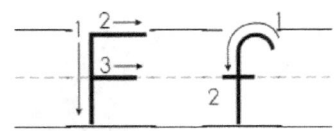

Trace the individual letters.
Then trace each animal name
and then say it aloud.

F F F F F F

F

f f f f f f f

f

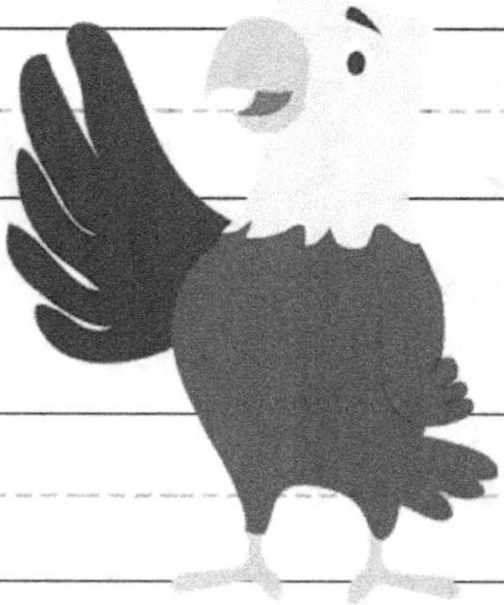

Falcon

Falcon Falcon

Fossa Fossa

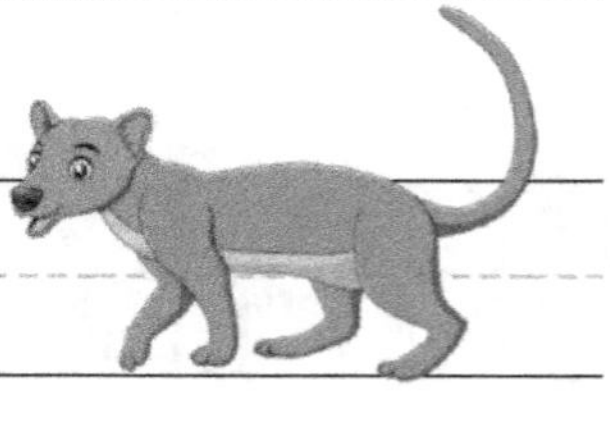

G g

Trace the individual letters.
Then trace each animal name
and then say it aloud.

G G G G G G

G

g g g g g g g g

g

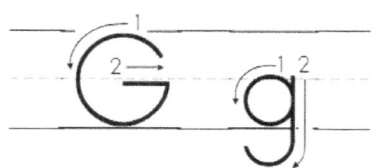

Gopher

Gopher Gopher

Gerbil

Trace the individual letters.
Then trace each animal name
and then say it aloud.

H o r s e

Horse Horse

Hyena Hyena

WRITING WITH THE DANGER TWINS

Trace the individual letters.
Then trace each animal name
and then say it aloud.

I i

I I I I I I

I

i i i i i i i i i

i

Indian Elephant

Indian Elephant

Indian Elephant

WRITING WITH THE DANGER TWINS

J j

Trace the individual letters.
Then trace each animal name
and then say it aloud.

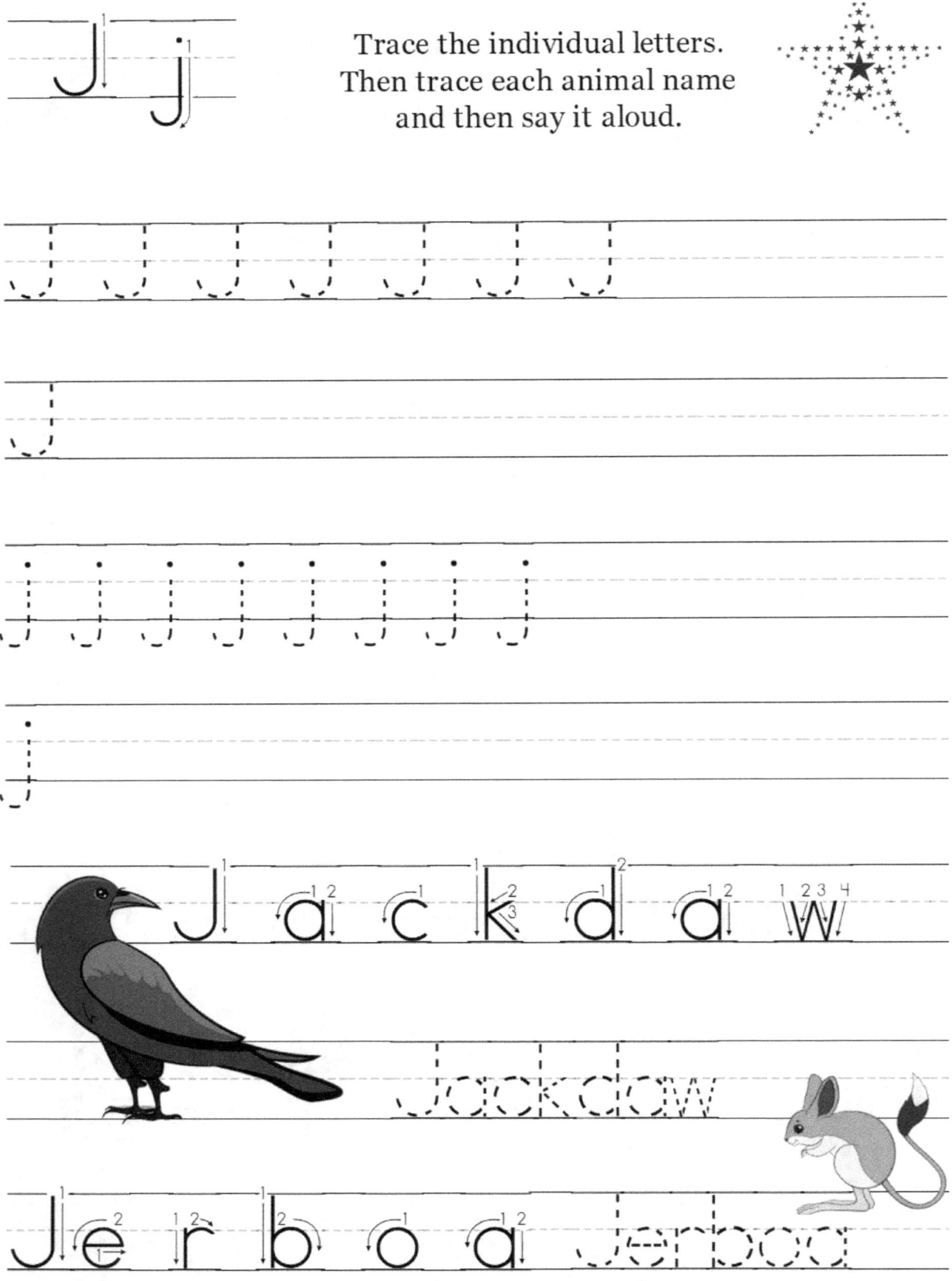

J J J J J J J J

J

j j j j j j j j

j

Jackdaw

Jackdaw

Jerboa Jerboa

66

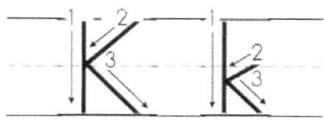

Trace the individual letters.
Then trace each animal name
and then say it aloud.

K K K K K K

K

K K K K K K K K

K

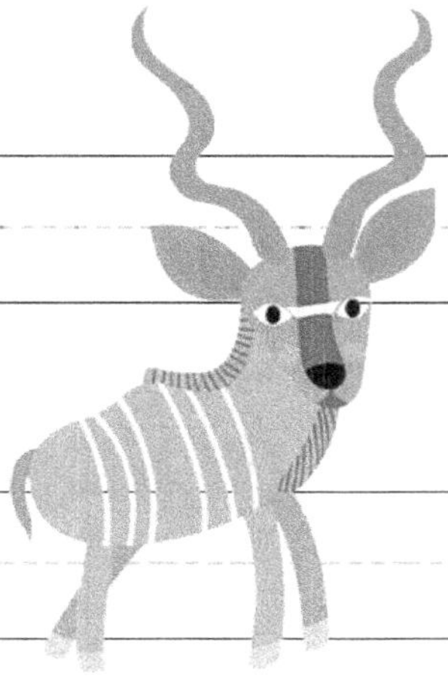

K u d o

Kudo   Kudo

Krill   Krill

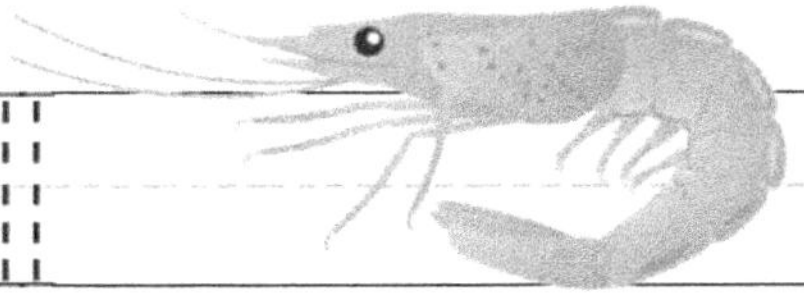

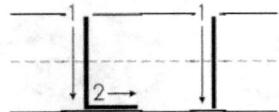

Trace the individual letters.
Then trace each animal name
and then say it aloud.

Lemur

Lemur Lemur

Lynx Lynx

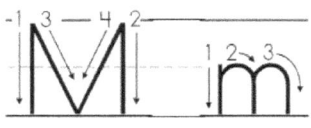

Trace the individual letters.
Then trace each animal name
and then say it aloud.

M M M M M

M

m m m m m m

m

Mule Mule

Mongoose

Mongoose

69

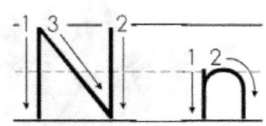

Trace the individual letters.
Then trace each animal name
and then say it aloud.

N N N N N N

N

n n n n n n n n

n

Nyala

Nyala Nyala

Newt Newt

WRITING WITH THE DANGER TWINS

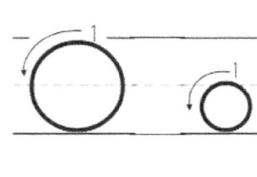

Trace the individual letters.
Then trace each animal name
and then say it aloud.

O O O O O

O

o o o o o o o

o

O c e l o t

Ocelot Ocelot

O t t e r Otter

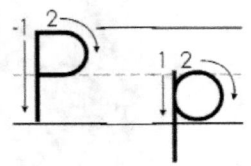

Trace the individual letters.
Then trace each animal name
and then say it aloud.

P P P P P P P

P

P P P P P P

P

Platypus

Platypus Platypus

Pug Pug Pug

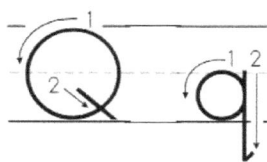

Trace the individual letters.
Then trace each animal name
and then say it aloud.

Q Q Q Q Q Q Q

Q

q q q q q q q

q

Queen Bee

Queen Bee

Quoll Quoll

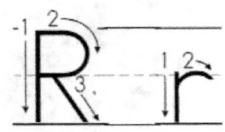

Trace the individual letters.
Then trace each animal name
and then say it aloud.

R R R R R R R

R

r r r r r r r

r

Reindeer

Reindeer Reindeer

Robin Robin

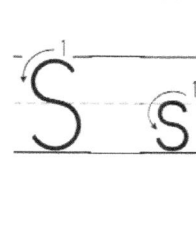

S s

Trace the individual letters.
Then trace each animal name
and then say it aloud.

S S S S S S

S

s s s s s s s

s

Seagull

Seagull Seagull

Snake Snake

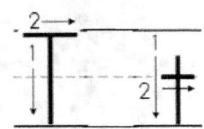

Trace the individual letters.
Then trace each animal name
and then say it aloud.

T T T T T T

T

t t t t t t t t

t

Tarpon Tarpon

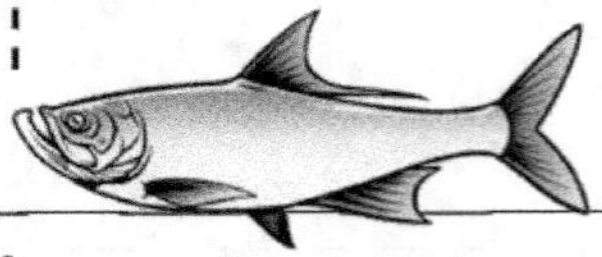

Tortoise

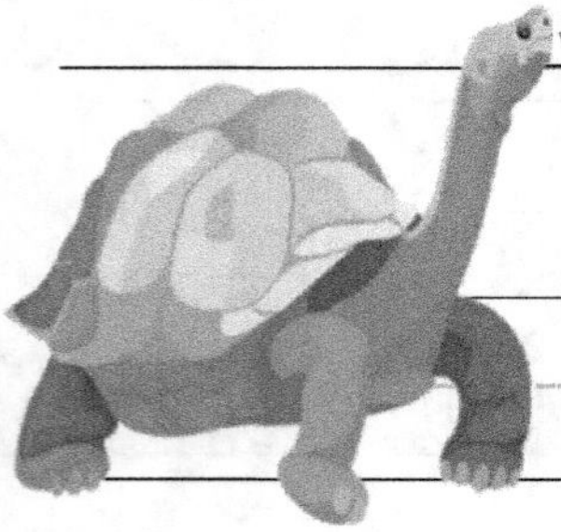

Tortoise Tortoise

U u

Trace the individual letters.
Then trace each animal name
and then say it aloud.

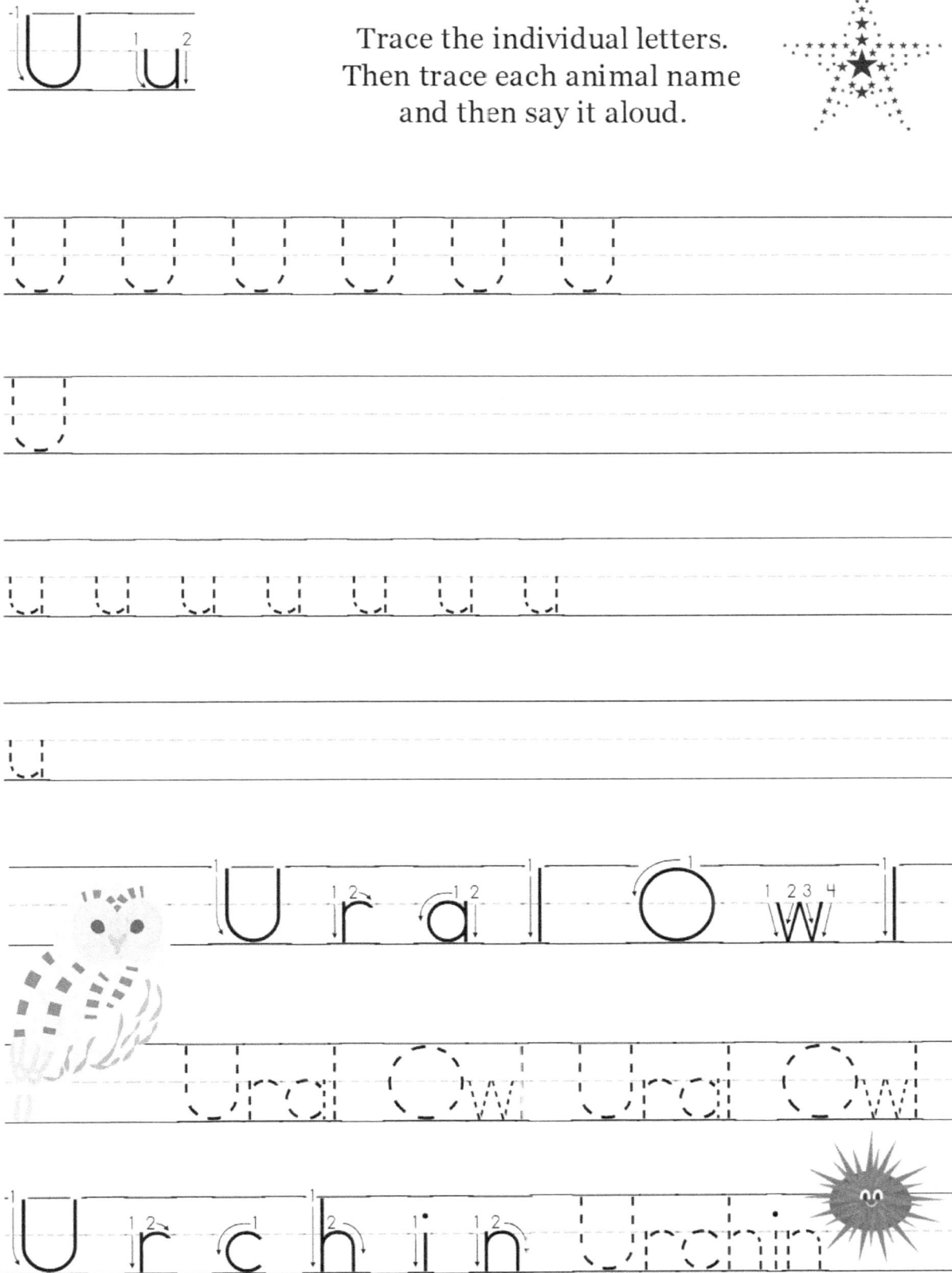

U U U U U U

U

u u u u u u

u

Ural Owl

Ural Owl Ural Owl

Urchin Urchin

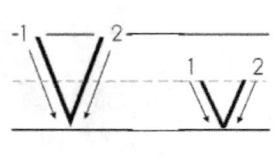

Trace the individual letters.
Then trace each animal name
and then say it aloud.

V V V V V V V V

V

V V V V V V V V

V

Vampire Bat

Vampire Bat

Vole Vole

78

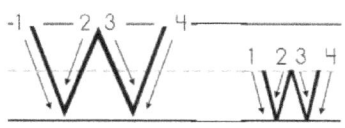

Trace the individual letters.
Then trace each animal name
and then say it aloud.

W W W W

W

w w w w w w w

w

Walrus

Walrus Walrus

Woodpecker

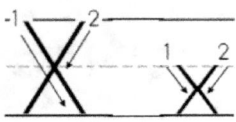

Trace the individual letters.
Then trace each animal name
and then say it aloud.

X X X X X X X

X

X X X X X X X X

X

Xiphias

Xiphias Xiphias

Xenops Xenops

WRITING WITH THE DANGER TWINS

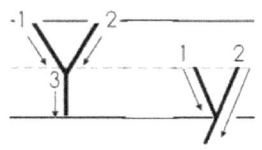

Trace the individual letters.
Then trace each animal name
and then say it aloud.

Y Y Y Y Y Y Y

Y

y y y y y y y

y

Yakutian

Yakutian

Yakutian

WRITING WITH THE DANGER TWINS

Z z Trace the individual letters. Then trace each animal name and then say it aloud.

Z Z Z Z Z Z Z Z

Z

z z z z z z z z

z

Zebra Finch

Zebra Finch

Zebra Finch

82

BONUS WORDS FROM THE DANGER TWINS

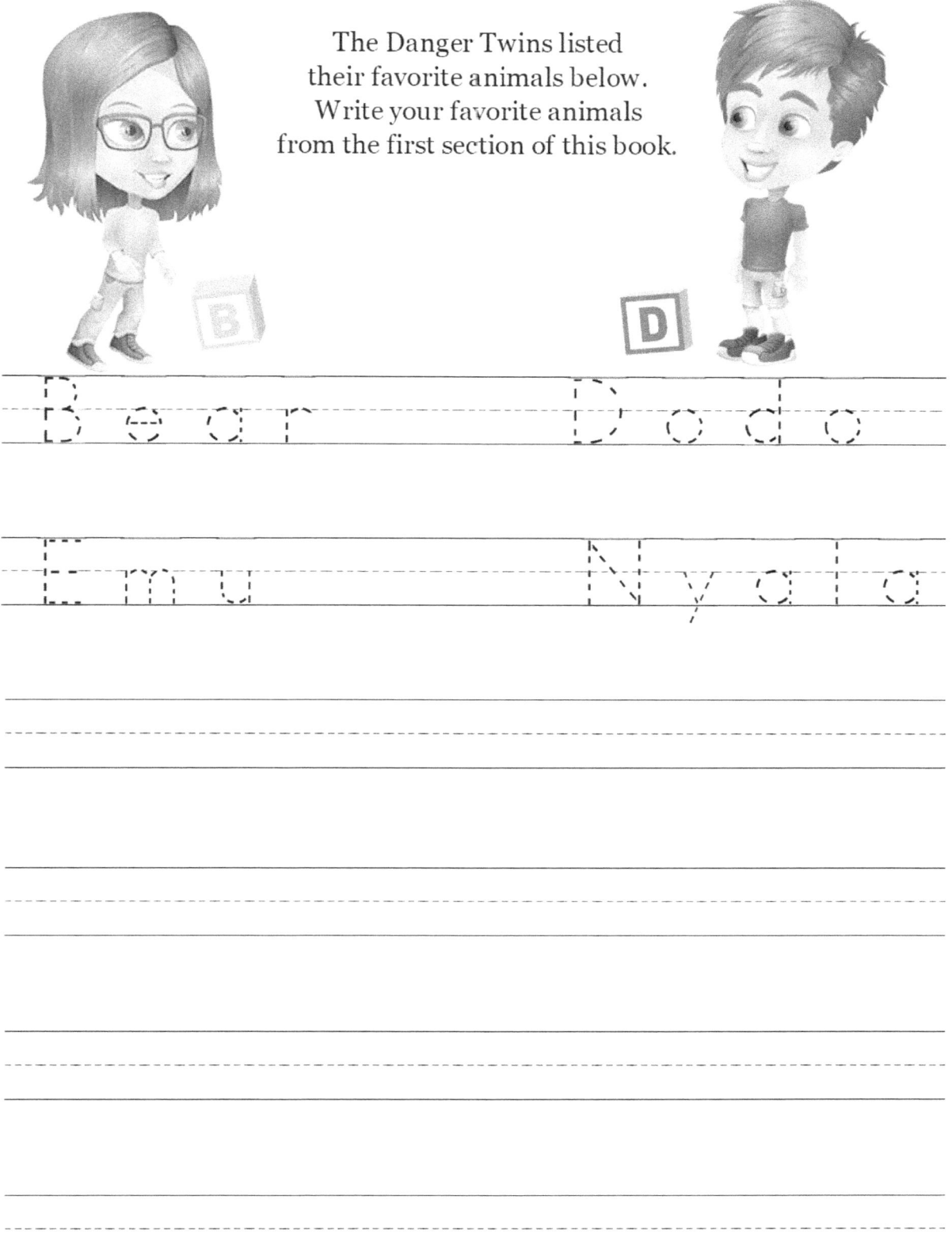

The Danger Twins listed their favorite animals below. Write your favorite animals from the first section of this book.

Bear   Dodo

Emu   Nyala

theDangerTwins.com

www.ingramcontent.com/pod-product-compliance
Lightning Source LLC
Chambersburg PA
CBHW081007120626
46546CB00010B/3045

* 9 7 8 1 9 5 6 5 4 7 0 4 7 *